Prophetic Wedding Planning Manual/Workbook

Prophetic Wedding Planning Manual/Workbook

Given to Minister Tommy & Evangelist Rosalind Willis
By the Holy Spirit
3-16-10
Foundational Scripture: Romans 4:17-20

Minister Tommy & Evangelist Rosalind Willis

Library of Congress Control Number:		2011906447
ISBN:	Hardcover	978-1-4628-6169-9
	Softcover	978-1-4628-6168-2
	Ebook	978-1-4628-6170-5

This book was printed in the United States of America.

To order additional copies of this book, contact:
Xlibris Corporation
1-888-795-4274
www.Xlibris.com
Orders@Xlibris.com
94932

CONTENTS

DEDICATION

This manual is dedicated first to our Lord and Savior Jesus Christ. Second, to our beautiful jewels Terrance, Takisha, Tommy Jr., James, Veranna, and Aaliyah. Third, our parents with honor and respect; Leon and Barbara Fields, Elder Bennie and Rita Clay, and our families; which have been a very important part of helping us to be molded for this vision.

Last but not least, to the Pastors and ministers that have labored in prayer and love to see this vision come to pass, in particular Pastor and First Lady Sherley and our Agape Love Family we are an extension of Agape Love Ministries. To Pastor and First Lady King and Galilee Baptist Church our local church family for accepting us and supporting us in ministry you all are truly appreciated and we love ya'll. To all of our Prophetic Wedding Planning students, we are very honored and humbled that the Lord brought each one of you across our path. We do not take it lightly. You all have deposited something into the both of us and we thank the Lord for all of you, for it is your hunger that dictated the anointing. Thank you all for the gift of giving us YOU! We pray that this manual is used as a point of reference to help navigate you all into the relationship, covenant, and marriage that God preordained for each of you to have, in Jesus Name!

The Vision of Prophetic Wedding Planning

Is to equip the men and women of God with the tools to prepare and walk in faith. As you walk in this faith, you will be prepared to receive the full manifestation of the promises and purposes for your lives. This is not just a wedding or marriage physically, but spiritually first! Before we are able to embrace any relationship we must develop a relationship with Christ. We must be married to His promises before we can understand or embrace our physical spouse. The actual wedding is an expression of the promises of God.

Now Faith—Hebrews 11:1

This is a prophetic class taught by the Holy Spirit working through his vessels.

FOREWORD

On May 24, 2004 I had the pleasure of meeting Rosalind Willis, at the Summer Institute for future global Leaders in the Caribbean St. Thomas V.I. What a dynamic connection; not only on a physical level but more so on a spiritual one. What a unique lady as she embraces herself, her truth, and her spirituality with such grace and finesse. Rosalind explained to me & others that our meeting was not just for Business Leadership but preparation as Spiritual Leaders. She stated that God was preparing me for marriage & my purpose here on earth was bigger than what I had realized. We had so much in common & our lives seemed to mirror each other, especially in our career choices.

I've known Tommy Willis for a little under a year however, I feel as if I've known him forever. There's a level of comfort when I speak to him, just as if I am talking with Rosalind. I don't see this couple as two for they are now one, therefore the trust, respect and love I have for Rosalind is the same that I have for Tommy.

In approximately two months it will make seven years that I've known Rosalind and so much of what she stated in 2004 have already manifested in my life. As God has truly been preparing me for marriage; Prophetic Wedding Planning couldn't have been written at a better time. Marriage is a Spiritual journey and it should not be taken likely. Marriage is Ministry and the meaning of this is to serve, that service begins at home, in which you demonstrate Christ perfect Love at all times. Christian marriage is not a contract, but rather a covenant relationship in which a man and a woman are united together as one in order to accomplish God's purpose for their lives. To know God is to know self; and once that perfect union is formed & you understand your purpose here on earth the ultimate goal is to do the will of God. God is utilizing your mate to help form the heart of Christ inside of you. God is providing that help here on earth wherein you can become the best of you and die to flesh daily. Marriage is such a big step and a lifelong commitment, the purpose of this book is to assist the reader on who, what, when, where, why & how to spiritually prepare you & your mate on this wonderful journey.

Both Rosalind and I knew about each other's fascination for writing from when we 1ˢᵗ met. However, we have recently realized that we are once again aligned by publishing our books around the same time. Introducing Rosalind's and Tommy's 1ˢᵗ book on "Prophetic Wedding planning," which emphasizes this couples journey and the visions, preparations and much more towards their destiny. My 1ˢᵗ book the "Power of Love," which is a compilation of Love Poetry inspired by my 1ˢᵗ true Love and my 2ⁿᵈ upcoming book on Inspirational Poetry—"Some spiritual lessons on my Faith & Journey"

Thanks Rosalind and Tommy Willis for allowing me the honor to write this Foreword in your very 1ˢᵗ book. Congratulations, many Blessings on your union and on all your future endeavors. It has been my pleasure preparing this Foreword. I know that all the readers will learn and grow from The Prophetic Wedding Manual and all your books to follow.

—Belinda Phillips

CHAPTER ONE

Our Spiritual Relationship
"The foundation of it all"

Tommy's Revelation

When Rosalind and I "Self" got married we already had that spiritual foundation. First of all; we had Jesus Christ in our lives above all else. Second, we had that kind of relationship between ourselves since we were teenagers that weren't in the physical realm but the spiritual. We were happy just to be in one another's presence. I knew where Ruth was coming from in Chapter 1:16 when she told Naomi, "Entreat me not to leave the, or to return from following after thee; for whither thou goes I will go, and where thou lodgest, I will lodge, thy people shall be my people, and thy God my God."

You see, when I first laid eyes on Rosalind she was the most beautiful girl I'd ever seen! But it went way past her physical attributes; it was her spirit man or "woman" that drew me to her. We served the same God because the first time I saw her was at church and we even sung in the same choir. Where she was is where I always wanted to be, and it was the same with her.

I don't remember asking her to be my girlfriend we were just, "IS". We felt right together. It took her mother to justify what we were, an "item".

I was like a deer caught in headlights. Mrs. Fields called me unto her yard and asked me point blank, 'was I going out with her daughter?' I didn't know whether to lie or tell her the truth; I was scared to death because Rosalind already had told me beforehand that her mom didn't allow her to date. My physical man wanted to lie to Mrs. Fields, but my spiritual man won out and I told her the truth. Which was the right thing to do because she gave me her blessing, with a, "You better do right by my daughter." And of course my response was, "Yes, Ma'am." And I am still sticking by my word to this day.

What made our relationship strong and have meaning is that I accepted her for the person she was and she accepted me for the person I was and we didn't have to discuss what was right or wrong in our relationship. It was that respect level on both sides and we did what the bible said do, "no sex before marriage" and we were content in being in each other's presence and kept our relationship on a spiritual basis instead of physical; which made our foundation all the more strong.

Rosalind's Revelation
"To Know Me Is To Love Me"

We cannot truly love a person if we do not really know them or ourselves. Christ is Love and the only way to truly know love is to know Jesus for he is love! In this life we all come from different backgrounds, religions, cultures and upbringing. Society as a whole has tried to mold us into the image of the world and its standards. As a Christian with a relationship with Jesus Christ we should always express our spiritual relationship through our everyday lives. When we interact with others we should allow that love or relationship with Christ Jesus to be spread abroad to the people we encounter. The problem with the world today is that we have allowed everything except for Jesus Christ to be in position or authority over us. We have the wrong and unstable foundation one that is uncertain and leaves us with doubt! Until we allow ourselves to know Jesus Christ nothing else will ever matter. If the foundation is wrong and unstable the house will not stand. The first time a real storm comes, the house will be destroyed because it is built on uncertainty and instability. In relationships, marriages, and partnerships we try to build on the wrong foundation and wonder why it does not last. How can I love you if I do not know you, better yet if I don't know me how can I love you? To know me is to love me, but who am I? The greatest gift of all from our Father is Jesus and until we receive that gift we have no foundation. I believe that when God created our mates for us and us for them he considered everything. Our natural spouse is supposed to be a reflection of Jesus Christ and so are we. The word of God tells us that men (husbands) are to love their wife as Christ loved the church and gave his life for it. (Ephesians 5:22) Here is just a little taste of the fruit that God has brought forth from this union:

(excerpt from our book, *It's All About Destiny: The Path To The Promise*) "*Wow, I do not really know where to start so I guess I will start at the beginning; only problem is I really don't know where that is! See Tommy and I never really started; we just were!*

"We are moving", Daddy said, as he walked in the front door from work one afternoon in Post TX . . . He never asked me out we just was. We always fit together from day one. " Wow, I am so excited about what He is doing in this season! Stay tuned . . .

Our Spiritual Relationship-Ruth Chapter 1-4
Spiritual Relationship

1. What kind of relationship did Ruth and Orpah have with Naomi and what were the differences?

    _____

    _____

2. Why do you think that Ruth trusted Naomi and stayed close to her?

    _____

    _____

3. Can you have a spiritual relationship with a person that does not know Jesus Christ?

    _____

    _____

4. Do you think motives can be a hindrance in your spiritual relationship?

    _____

    _____

5. Is there a price to pay to obtain a spiritual relationship with Jesus?

    _____

    _____

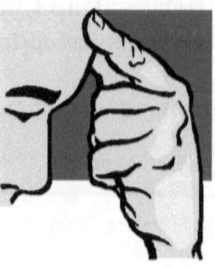

Take a minute here to reflect on your own spiritual foundation and ask yourself the question, who am I?

_____

_____

_____

_____

_____

_____

_____

_____

_____

_____

_____

_____

_____

CHAPTER TWO

Intimacy
Spiritual and Natural

Tommy's Revelation

It took years of trials and going through with past relationships with other women, friends, or family to truly comprehend what the word intimacy truly means. I am going to use the first part of verse 6 of 1st Kings Chapter 3 of the New Living Translation version; it says, "Solomon replied, "You showed faithful love to your servant my father, David because he was honest and true and faithful to you." You see, Solomon was speaking to the Lord here.

God loved David and showed him favor. Not because of anything else except because David was honest, true and faithful to the Lord. That is how we should be to the Lord in all our endeavors. Having an intimate relationship with Him, then everything or everyone we may encounter will pan out because we are intimate with the Lord on a spiritual basis not natural. By having that type of relationship with the Lord it should spill over into our marriage and your spouse should not ever wander or have any doubt that you love her or him.

When I look back at the only intimate relationship I ever truly had was with Rosalind. As she describes it best "Into Me See". I didn't know her in the natural or flesh until we were married. But she knew me then and knows me now better than anyone in this world. I only let her see every part of me. My weaknesses, my strengths, fears, etc . . . We have that spiritual kind of intimacy that surpasses the natural in every aspect. She have always saw me naked as I saw her; figuratively speaking. We saw the inner most part of each other that no one else saw or see. It has to be that trust, deep understanding and that faith in Christ in that person for you to truly be open with.

If you are in the natural (flesh), it can cloud your judgment what true intimacy really is. Having sex with a person is not true intimacy at all, but an imposter to make you think you are on that intimacy plane with your mate or whatever title you have for him or her. Making love to your spouse shouldn't only be in natural form (flesh), but in the spiritual form as well.

As I said before, I didn't truly know Rosalind in the natural form until we were married, but I have made love to her since we were teenagers. I made love to her mind by stimulating it and her heart by penetrating it and cherishing it and going to levels that no other has ever been but me. And she has return that same kind of love, because we are "Self". To this day our intimacy in the spiritual that we share is far greater than the natural that we share.

Rosalind's Revelation
"Into Me See"

This is a very personal, yet liberating revelation "Into Me See"; true intimacy. How can I be intimate with anyone if I have not allowed God to reveal to me who I am? In life I experienced years of jumping through hoops trying to make everyone happy or just to be accepted by everyone else. When I found myself staring in the mirror yet I did not know who that person was in the mirror looking back at me. The worst deception is self-deception. (1 Corinthians 13:12) I could paint on a smile when I felt like screaming inside. I knew how to convince anyone of anything I wanted them to believe, but in the end I only deceived myself. I did not know who I was, and had no true identity.

I went from relationship to relationship trying to find in a man what only God could give me; "*true intimacy.*" When we can stand alone with ourselves and be naked and not ashamed (Genesis 2:25) only then can we allow our mate to see into us! The reason that I am so deeply in love with my husband is he knows me; the good, the bad and the ugly and he still loves me unconditionally!

The word of the Lord talks about the kind of respect that Sarah had for Abraham; she called him Lord (1 Peter 3:3-6)! Now I know there are those of you that are questioning that, just as I used to. I was one of those women that when I first read that passage thought, "I don't see that." Now I understand exactly what she was talking about. Just think about it; if God says to men that they ought to love their wives as Christ loved the church and gave his life for her, then how much more should we love our husbands as the reflection of

Christ? When I am in worship I get lost in the presence of the Lord because of our intimacy that we share. The only other intimacy that even comes close to that intimate experience is being in the presence of my love; "Tommy Wayne Willis Sr." I have always been content and completely at peace just being in his presence. "INTO ME SEE "means to look deeper than what is on the outside of me like my hips, lips, and fingertips. Deeper than what I am saying to you in the natural, but in my spirit. Know this—we are more than flesh, but we also as Christ are spirit because he is in us and us in him. I now know that My Love touched me in the spirit before he ever touched me in the flesh and that my dear ones, is the" into me see" place. Now I must explain something to you all; I was married three times to the same man before Tommy and I were married. I would constantly beat myself up because the marriage failed, time and time again. I would always tell myself it was my entire fault. I was not skinny enough or I was too loud. I even went through a phase of blaming myself for being too saved and you know the phrase *"so heavenly bound that I was no earthly good"*. I continually prayed, fasted and sought the Lord about my marriage.

I know God hates divorce and I do also and coming from a household where my father and mother have been together all my life I had no point of reference for divorce. The worse thing in the world to experience in life is spiritual rejection. Yes, I said it, spiritual rejection; you can't apologize for who God has created you to be in. When you are not accepted in the spirit sometimes we find ourselves trying to apologize for something not in our power to control. We marry for the wrong reasons and with hidden agendas. When it is all said and done we are left with ourselves and the truth of why we said the words "I DO"! We cannot marry our assignments or someone that we were meant to be friends with or pray for. Perversion comes in many forms not just sexual. If we are not completely real with ourselves then we cannot be real with others. My ex-husband and I are now civil towards one another, but we had to go through years of heartache and take our kids and families through pain because we were not true with ourselves or each other.

It is truly important to know what you want in a mate. You need to discuss your backgrounds, religious upbringing, and most of all your relationship with Christ Jesus. There is a gigantic difference between a person that is simply religious and one that has a relationship. When you have experienced intimacy with Christ Jesus and you have a revelation of who you are in him, you cannot be simply religious anymore, because; *"He whom the son sets free is free in deed*!" Religion is from a knowledge base "what I know about Christ Jesus", but a relationship is from the spirit base "I know Jesus Christ and I am his and he is mine! Into me see! Can you see Jesus when you see me or can you only see him in what I say and not what I do? That is the question today. The church have become filled with wonderful actors and actresses, but when they returned to their everyday patterns, the same individuals look nothing like the part they played on Sunday morning. Some don't even say hello to you when you see them in the grocery store. We have to do better as examples of Jesus Christ and his love! We have to be the walking, talking, dancing, preaching, teaching, loving, and working word of the Lord.

Before I could begin to accept my purpose in life and understand my destiny I had to forgive myself for divorce and then forgive my ex-husband! I could not even enter into the presence of the Lord for years without feeling so ashamed because my marriage had failed, time and time again even though I wanted it because of the false picture I had painted in my mind. I cried day after day and prayed and forgave and turned, but divorce still came! I had to stop and really look around to see what was still standing in my life, and then make a decision for myself that I would not allow the enemy to steal another thing from me. I had to accept the fact that I am not God and I cannot change anyone or make them love me better. I cannot change myself, only God could change me!

I truly do believe that the Lord has a mate for each one of us; that He has created us women for. The problem is we become too anxious and move out of place and go to find the man instead of allowing him to find us (Proverbs 18:22)! We do not see anywhere in the word where Adam was brought to and presented to Eve. Quite the opposite, she was created for and presented to Adam as a gift from God (Genesis 2:22). Adam was able to look at Eve and see himself. (Genesis 2:23) Adam saw into Eve; he knew her name and he had always been with her for she was always inside of him! *Woman now bone of my bones and flesh of my flesh*! He knew her because she came out of him! Isn't it something how Majestic God is and his awesome wisdom, far beyond words? Now all living comes out of woman so Adam was the first man that delivered out of himself a woman. She was taken from his rib which is to protect the vital organs especially the heart.

As I remember, with each of my children I had to be given medication to help induce my labor because they did not want to be rushed out of my womb when the doctor said it was time. I remember going to sleep and waking up in full labor. All of my children were delivered naturally. The word of God says that the Lord caused a deep sleep to fall upon Adam I believe that was God performing the first surgery. He is all and everything to know him is to experience him in every aspect of his greatness. He was the anesthesiologist, the surgeon, and also the nurse! He is and always will be God; there is none like him! There is no way around Jesus and no way to the Father God, but through Jesus. God the Father, the Son and the Holy Ghost—they are one! You cannot separate a man from his word just as you cannot separate God from his word (Jesus) for the word of the Lord says in St. John 1:1, "In the beginning was the Word, and the Word was with God, and the Word was God". The Word also lets us know in John 1:14 that "The word was made flesh, and dwelt among us, and we beheld his Glory and the only begotten of the Father, full of grace and truth. John 1:10, 11 say, "Christ

Jesus was in the world and the world was made by him, and the world knew him not". He came unto his own, and his own received him not. I was liberated the day I received the revelation that if Jesus was rejected by his own what makes me think I would not face rejection? I am not talking about someone not accepting you because of your size, your tone, or some other physical characteristic, but I am talking about spiritual rejection. When someone that you love and would lay down your life for; turns again and again and walks away from you to embrace another way; it hurts more than words can ever express. I am talking about Jesus who came to die for the sins of the entire world; even me and you. "Yet when I was in my sins Christ died for me". I used to read this particular passage of scripture and get teary eyed; just the thought that I was not even a concept in my mother's mind at that time. But, the revelation that the Holy Spirit revealed to me is that in the Spirit realm there is no time the way we calculate it today. The word of the Lord says to be absent from the body is to be present with the Lord. It also lets us know that God is omnipresent. He is everywhere at the same time. When Christ Jesus died on the cross for my sins I was there already in the spirit because we are in him and him in us! Nothing can separate us from the love of God and nothing can snatch us from him—we belong to him!

Intimacy-Spiritual and Natural-1Kings 3:16-28 "Two Women"

1. Is intimacy something that others can see?

_____

_____

2. How can we experience true intimacy with Christ Jesus?

_____

_____

3. How can we experience true intimacy with our mate?

_____

_____

4. How did the two harlots show a connection with their babies and what were the differences?

_____

_____

5. How can you take the two actions displayed by the harlots and compare them to your spiritual and natural intimacy?

_____

_____

Take a minute here to reflect on what true INTIMACY is to you.

_____

_____

_____

_____

_____

_____

_____

_____

_____

_____

_____

_____

_____

_____

_____

_____

CHAPTER THREE

How to Identify Counterfeits
Spiritually Discerning

Tommy's Revelation

Rosalind and I didn't ever fall out of love. But, as she moved back to her hometown when we were teenagers we decided to just remain friends. By then I already had a template of what "realness" was by being in a relationship with her. With her it was always real. We both had our best interests for one another at heart. We knew where the other stood on certain things at all times and didn't cross those boundaries. We were honest and truthful to one another and communication was the key. We still stand by that to this day.

At a young age we talked about marriage, what type of wedding we wanted, the house, the kids, etc. Speaking for myself, when I looked ahead I had no doubts that I wanted to spend the rest of my life with her. If you have any doubts about the person you are going to make your "lifetime" mate you need to listen to that inner voice because he or she may be a counterfeit.

Never, I mean NEVER settle. Don't try to mold a person into what you want him or her to be like. Only God is the best of molders. And if that person is in the world, eventually he or she is going to do their master's business, which is Satan. If you are having problems in the relationship before marriage, never think that by marrying that person that it will change that person for the better. Only God can do that if that person really wants to change.

"Real" is a giver, not a taker. When *Self* (Rosalind) and I bump heads, it's only because we both want to do for each other. It's hard for me to just sit back and let her just serve me because I want to serve and pamper her all the time. She has to remind me sometimes to let her do her wifely duties. My greatest joy comes from when I am serving my Queen. I know I can be irksome at times because she wants to do the same for me. She is the type of woman of God, whom would just serve me all the time if I let her and not expect anything in return. If I allowed that, it would make me a counterfeit, a taker. I am so honored in serving my Lord and my Wife.

Rosalind's Revelation

Many of you at some time in your life have experienced someone that acted like your friend, talked like they were your friend and when trouble came they could not be found.

I was just watching an episode on T.V. of a court show and there was a man and his wife getting a divorce because the wife lost 200 lbs. and the husband said he was not attracted to her anymore. As the show continued they took turns telling the judge what they did and did not like about each other. Then it is discovered that the husband is having an affair with his wife's good friend from church. She comes out and we, the television audience gets to see the devastation in the eyes of the wife as she realizes that this woman was not her friend all along.

I personally have no problem with someone that comes out and says I just don't like you, I can take that because then I know where we stand. What I have a problem with is a person that says to you I love you or you're my best friend and then they stab you in the back. This is one type of counterfeit.

When a person do not have their own identity they try to copy yours, and we all know a copy is simply that, a copy. When you place the real thing beside the copy they look alike, may even act alike, but the real will always shine through.

Definition of a counterfeit as defined in the Webster's dictionary is: made in imitation; not genuine; forged. Fraud, sham, bogus, make believe, insincere, artificial, fake, reproduction of the original.

The counterfeit does not produce or cannot produce, it can only reproduce. It has to operate from something that is already real. It has no point of originality because it is only a copy of the real thing.

Matthew 7:15-20 speaks of these counterfeits:

Verse 15 says, "Beware of false prophets, which come to you in sheep's clothing, but inwardly they are ravening wolves."

Verse 16 says, "Ye shall know them by their fruits. Do men gather grapes of thorns, or figs of thistles."

Verse 17 says, "Even so every good tree bringeth forth evil fruit."

Verse 18 says, "A good tree cannot bring forth evil fruit, neither can a corrupt tree bring forth good fruit."

Verse 19 says, "Every tree that bringeth not forth good fruit is hewn down, and cast into the fire."

Verse 20 says, "Wherefore by their fruits ye shall know them."

(The Holy Bible: King James Version. 2000).

The only way to identify them is by examining their fruit. Remember they can only copy, they can't produce. The fruit is bad and corrupt. A counterfeit does not have unconditional agape love. The counterfeit can't operate in the truth. The work of the Lord and the Holy Spirit will uncover the counterfeit and will help you to spiritually identify them.

The counterfeit is only there to detour you from the real thing. But God uses the counterfeits for your good. I thank God for every counterfeit that I ever came in contact with because of them I know how to appreciate the real thing! You can look at the counterfeit like a buffer, they rub you the wrong way, but in the long run you come out smoother. It might hurt but it will help you in the long run.

Discerning Counterfeits
Matthew 7:15-20

1. What did the Lord says, about discerning counterfeits?

_____

_____

2. How can you discern a counterfeit in a relationship?

_____

_____

3. Can a counterfeit help you be a better judgment of characters? Why or Why not.

_____

_____

4. How do you know if you are a counterfeit?

_____

_____

5. In what way can you identify a counterfeit?

_____

_____

Take a minute here to reflect on your current or former relationships. Fruit inspect and allow the Holy Spirit to reveal to you the counterfeits in your life so that you will know how to pray about them.

_____

_____

_____

_____

_____

_____

_____

_____

_____

_____

_____

_____

_____

CHAPTER FOUR

How do I know he or she is the One?
Characteristics of the Promise

Tommy's Revelation
"The Real Thing"

We can say all day that we can feel it in every fiber or our beings that he or she is the one. But, until we are in order with God and walking in Jesus Christ can we truly feel that we have found that right person for us.

We did a demonstration in our Prophetic Wedding class in the session of how to deal with the counterfeit: We had four people come up front and we had the real Coca Cola and a generic brand of Cola; we also had the real Dr. Pepper and a generic brand of Dr. Pepper. We gave each a real Cola or Dr. Pepper and then the fake Cola and Dr. Pepper. We put them in paper cups so they wouldn't know what they were drinking and all had them in each hand. We had them drink from the right hand first and then the left; explaining which one they thought was real and which one was the generic brand as well as which flavor were they. Taster #1 was exactly right on the flavors as well as which one was real and which one was fake. Taster #2 had the flavors mixed up even though he was right on which one was real and which one was generic. Taster #3 had the flavors right, but said that both was generic even though he had the "real" Coca Cola in his right hand. And taster #4 had the flavors mixed up as well as which one was real and which one was generic.

The demonstration showed scenarios in how relationships can be. Lord knows; it happens more often than not on all four accounts. We come across people that we think are the real thing or "The One" and they turn out to be fake. Or we had the real thing and didn't know that person was real until we find ourselves in a relationship with a fake, a phony, or water down version of what we once had. The real thing touches every area of your being so that you won't go lacking in anything. I am speaking from a spiritual standpoint. If you are sleeping with that person before marriage, you may not be able to discern the difference if he or she is the real or fake because you are in the natural (flesh) and not in the spiritual or will of God.

I went through a few relationships before and after Rosalind and all others didn't compare. Maybe because I was in a natural (flesh) relationship with them and wasn't in **spiritual order** with God. With Rosalind at 15 years old I knew she was the "real thing" and we dealt with each other on a spiritual level and it was never flesh or perverted.

God did bless Ishmael and his descendants, but Isaac was the promise. I believe there is someone out there promised to each and every one of us. Predestined and preordained by God. Because God says, He cares about what we care about, but first we have to do everything in order to receive that promise. And I know the Lord blessed me with the one person that I knew was "the One" for me. Rosalind and I used to say some 23 years ago that we were going to be married. But, speaking for myself, I wasn't lining up to God's will or walking with Christ so I had to drink a lot of generic brand sodas, so to speak, before I received my promise. I went through a lot of trials, tribulations, heartache and pain because of my actions and behavior. But once I started to be in order with God was I truly blessed to taste the "real thing" once again! And that is having my Baby back into my life after all of these years. Not only as my girlfriend, but as my WIFE! God is truly good!

Rosalind's Revelation

No one knows who the one is when they are born into this world. The key to knowing that he or she is the one is by number one, knowing the difference by identifying between love and lust. We wonder why divorce rates are at the highest level, and the answer is in the question "What is Marriage?" In this day and time with all the issues that are in our world today concerning marriages such as, same-sex marriages, and transgender marriages. God Ordained marriage and he created it; we must remember no matter how many ways the world try to change the original form, the definition will always be the same. God created Adam and Eve and they became one flesh, male and female he created them. (Genesis 1:27). We must understand what God meant when he said it is not good for man to be alone. He looked in the garden at all that he had made, all the animals had a suitable mate but, Adam was alone. God in his loving, caring nature did not want Adam to be without a reflection of himself. He gave Adam seed and allowed him to plant inside Eve to reproduce natural fruit. One of things that I had to learn was how to appreciate my very own value. Value is something we do not hear about every day. We watch videos and television shows of young women being treated like sex objects instead of young ladies. We allow that same mindset to creep into our homes. When I begin to understand my value, I began to understand I am worth more than this. How many times have you witnessed a relationship on the outside where there is this beautiful man or woman that is connected with someone who treats him or her like trash? I was that woman more times than I can count on one hand. The problem was not the men, I was the problem. How can someone appreciate your value if you do not know how much you are worth yourself? It is like going into an expensive store with little or no money picking up valuable items and sitting them back down. Eventually because the sales agent knows the item is valuable will either approach you or send security to watch you. If you are a person that's known to have expensive taste and the salesperson knows that you have an eye for value he or she would try to sell you the item. I settled for less on many occasions because I did not know my very own value. In a healthy relationship your mate is supposed to build you up not tear you down. If there is no one in the world standing on your side your mate should always be.

To the men and women out there battling with your own value or worth, there are a few things you should try.

First, sit down and evaluate who you are and what you have to offer seek the Lord for this answer.

Second, write down the things that you love about yourself.

Third, write down the things that you dislike about yourself.

Fourth, embrace who you are and why you are you!

Fifth, allow the Lord to teach you the definition of your unique value.

You may find that you are a wonderful asset to any relationship. When you are true with yourself it is easy to be true with others. Once you get past this stage it will not be difficult to find the one or except the one for your life. When you come from a dysfunctional background it is hard to understand value. The norm to you may be very unmoral to your mate. It is important to get to know your mate so that you can begin to understand your differences. This makes for a better marriage.

Be friends first; know the individual in all facets of love. Experience your mate in every social way that you can without saying I do. By the time you get married you should know your mate and your mate should know you. The only thing that should wait until marriage is physical intimacy; it is only sacred and blessed on your wedding night. If you cannot stand to be alone or in public with your mate how can you be with them the rest of your life. If your mate is loud and you are quiet and you cannot stand loud people you may want to be honest with yourself, and question if this is really the one? If the lists of things you like about your self are the list of things that your mate dislikes about you that is a red flag.

How can you receive a gift and never open it to see what it is? That is what we are doing when we do not get to know whom we are being connected with in the eye sight of God as our lifetime mates. A gift and never open it to see what it is? That is what we are doing when we do not get to know whom we are being connected with in the eye sight of God as our lifetime mates. If you are doubting if he or she is the one because of a long list of hurts that you have encountered at the hand of the mate that is a sign to STOP, turn around, and reroute! If you are being hurt in the relationship that is not God's plan for your life. The word of God says that he come that we may have life and that life more abundantly. (John 10:10). Being abused mentally or physically is not living that abundant life. Think about It, if we as parents get upset and want to protect our children from any kind of hurt, how much more does our Heavenly Father care for us? No, I am not saying go divorce your mate, I am saying seek the Lord for his Divine Will for your marriage and overall life!

Characteristics of the Promise
Genesis 17:18-21

1. Why did God establish the covenant with Isaac and not Ishmael?

    _____

    _____

2. How can you discern if the person that you are in a relationship with is right for you?

    _____

    _____

Take a minute to reflect on the person that you are with now. List the pros and cons of this person in every area that you think is important in a relationship. (Spiritually connected should be on the top of the list) After your list do you still think that they are the Real Thing?

Areas	Pros	Cons
Spiritually connected		

Are they the promise for your life time mate or the "Real Thing"? Why or why not?

_____

_____

_____

CHAPTER FIVE

Marriage and the Preparation
To the Promises

Rosalind's Revelation

To prepare to join yourself with the "One" for your lifetime mate can't be done in the natural (flesh). You have to have that spiritual foundation. You two have to study the Word together, you have to pray together, and you have to worship together. You have to let that person in, into your inner most thoughts, the awareness of your strengths as well as your weaknesses. You don't want to go into a marriage not truly knowing the other person. If you don't truly know that person, once you're in the marriage and then skeletons starts to come out of the closet. And then you might look at the individual as if they betrayed you and it starts to hinder your marriage and just maybe your walk with Christ.

If that starts to happen you can't point fingers at the other person all of the time because it is up to you to talk to that individual on levels that you wouldn't talk to anyone else because he or she is the one that is going to be you, "Self" as long as you are upon this earth. The best thing to do is pray and study the word with your mate, as well as worship with them. Tell each other what you want to accomplish in your union; your goals and ambitions and pray that the good Lord gives you both a sense of direction and purpose to do His will.

Tommy and I did just that and are doing it now. We have had a lot of confirmations in doing this Prophetic Wedding Planning class. We both know that we can't teach anything if we are not walking in it. Most of all we have to have the good Lord at the forefront of our walk. We talk about everything with each other and we definitely pray, study together, and worship together.

Let me start by saying, you cannot prepare yourself to be joined with the One; just allow God to process you through your walk in him. If you listen to the leading of the Holy Spirit you will not be misled. I had no idea through all of the hurt and pain I had encountered;it would have led me to such pleasure in marriage. The truth is I have always wanted Jesus and his best for me, I just did not know how to obtain it. When I moved out of the way and listened to the leading of the Holy Spirit he walked me into his best for my life.

The Lord will prepare you just as he did Esther in the bible. She was chosen in a time when on a normal day she would have not been in the count. She found favor with the King because of purpose. Esther went through purification and beautification treatments. Don't give up when you encounter a lot of hurt in your life just continue to seek the Lord and stay at his feet. Esther had to stand in the gap for her entire blood line. And the trap that the enemy set for her he literally fell in it himself. We do not have to sneak and slither our way to the top. If we just be still and wait on the Lord he will send your mate to you. I am a living witness. Tommy had to go through some years of preparation and process and so did I but, God and his timing allowed us to meet up in the place and time that he preordained for the both of us. Esther was chosen for her time to stand in the gap and I believe that Tommy and I were chosen for such a time as this to change a generation. When I first read the book of Esther I thought she was chosen as Queen by default, but now reading; the Holy Spirit revealed to me she was chosen by purpose. So don't be so quick to judge your situation because God has not forgotten about you and he is not slack at all concerning his promises. (Read complete book of Esther KJV)

Tommy's Revelation

As "Self" says, 'you have to prepare yourself with the "One" for your lifetime mate and it can't be done in the natural (flesh). You have to have that spiritual foundation.' Even though we were *first loves* God didn't bring us together until I was prepared for Rosalind. You see I had to be processed and molded just right to be Rosalind's husband.

Our flesh said that we were meant for each other, but spiritually we would have been unequally yoked. Rosalind is an Ordained Evangelist and Minister for over 15 years. While she was travailing and praising the one true God and our Lord and Savior Jesus Christ; I was proclaiming to be Muslim and not following the one who died for my sins. In John 14:6 Jesus said, "I am the way, the truth, and the life. No one comes to the Father except through me."

Until I found my way back to Christ and accepted Him back into my heart and life as my personal Savior was I ready for Rosalind into my life. As she stated above, we have to pray together as well as worship together as the Lord would have us to be. How can she be praying and worshipping Jesus and I am praying and giving alms to Muhammad? It would never have worked. Because I know I couldn't change her way of thinking and worshipping because she is not religious she has a *relationship* with Christ. I had to see the light and come out of the wilderness, so to speak. Thank God that I have. I now have that relationship with Christ that I've always wanted.

I watch my wife in all her endeavors and how she reacts to everyday life. She is my best teacher in this Christian walk. What more could a man ask for than to have a wife that he can share everything with, pray with and worship with. She is a person that I genuinely like and respect; not because she is my wife, but the Godly woman that she is. She is my best friend and confidant; that I tell all; the good, the bad, and the ugly. I don't want any open door ways. No one can ever go to my wife and tell her something about me (just to be messy), that she doesn't know about. Believe me; it has happened in our relationship. If you tell your wife or husband everything then the devil can't plant any seeds of doubt and cause trouble in your marriage.

You and your significant other should talk about everything that could be detrimental to your marriage if the information would come out after the marriage. That person should know you more than anyone else upon this earth. You two will be one; "Self".

Hebrews 13:4-Marriage should be held in Honor

1. What revelation do you get out of this scripture?

_____

_____

2. How do you prepare yourself for marriage?

_____

_____

3. Why do you think that praying and studying with your spouse is important?

_____

_____

4. Think of something that you feel is shameful, or you have guilt about that you haven't shared with your mate.

_____

_____

5. Can a marriage last if you are serving the Lord and your spouse is not? Why or Why Not?

_____

_____

Take a minute to reflect on preparing for marriage. What must you do as a child of God to make sure that you are prepared and ready to be that spouse that the other can depend on and lean on throughout your lives together?

_____

_____

_____

_____

_____

_____

_____

_____

_____

_____

_____

_____

_____

_____

_____

_____

_____

_____

CHAPTER SIX

Vows and the Vision of the Marriage
Divine Agreement

Tommy's Revelation

As you prepare for the marriage with your spouse you have to have a vision for your marriage and you need to discuss it with your mate, so there is anything that he or she is not in agreement with; you two can discuss it until there is one. If there is something that your spirit doesn't agree with, never ever compromise. I read book years ago that gave me the inspiration on my vows and I used his theme as we wrote our vows; the book was named "Raising Fences", by Michael Datcher. Rosalind and I wrote our own vows when we got married. I am going to write them out in this section and explain why I wrote them and what vision I had when I did write them:

"For as long as God continues to raise the morning sun, I will hold these vows sacred."-This was our main focus on both Rosalind and I vows, because if we can't do this one sentence right here than anything after this doesn't even matter. Because after this point any vow I write has to be kept wholeheartedly where my wife is concerned as long as I have breath and the good Lord blesses me to wake up each morning.

"**I vow** to love you with my mind, body, spirit. To be a caretaker of your inner woman and to keep your name in God's ear."-I was promising her that I will love her with every fiber of my being. And be there for her not only in the natural, but in the spiritual as well. And I will continue to pray for her health and her walk with Christ on a constant basis.

"**I vow** to be a productive confidant for your dreams and ambitions in life and to help bring them into reality. To challenge you as I challenge myself so that we may continuously produce good fruit."-I was promising her that I will be a good listener as well as a source for her to bring all her dreams and ambitions into fruition. And challenge her as well as myself to not get stagnant in life but to bring people to Christ, so that they may be of blessing to others and bring them into the fold.

"**I vow** to be an everlasting source for our children so that they may come to me for a sense of direction and guidance. And provide them with love, knowledge, and understanding."-I promise to be there for all our children whenever they need someone to listen so that they may vent, or they need advice on just experiences in what they are walking through. And I will continue to show them love, the knowledge and understanding of life and above all else be an example in my Christian walk.

"**I vow** to accept you, Self, Baby, my Beautiful Queen as my lifetime mate, to believe in you and toil with you; not only in our finest hours, but in the midst of adversity as well. So that our connection through life will be of love and the inner peace of being loved."-I promise to accept Rosalind as my wife until the good Lord calls us home. To believe in her and work with her not only in our best of times, but in times of trouble. In whatever we may face in life good or bad will bring us closer by knowing that I love her and the peace of knowing that my depth of the love I have for her; she has that same depth of love for me.

"**I vow** to serve you as well as accepting of being served. To respect your thoughts, your sense of self-worth, the Godly woman that the good Lord called you to be and the sanctity of our marriage that He has so graciously blessed us with."-I was promising her to serve her as well as letting her serve me as a husband and wife should serve one another for the rest of our lives upon this earth. To respect every part of her, the sanctity of our marriage, and above all else the Godly woman that she is.

"**I vow** to love you as Christ love the Church and gave His life for it."-I was promising her to love her unconditionally for the rest of my life.

Take a minute to write your vows if not your vows,
then the vision for your marriage.

_____

_____

_____

_____

_____

_____

_____

_____

_____

_____

_____

_____

_____

_____

_____

_____

_____

_____

"**I vow** to love you as I love myself. Because you are a reflection of me and I am a reflection of you. We are One in Christ Jesus . . . We are Self"-I was promising to love her as I love myself because as husband and wife we are a union, in the name of the Father, Son, and Holy Ghost. And as One in this life, not only in the natural, but in the spiritual and our walk with Christ has to be on one accord at all times.

"**I vow** to always be there for you in good times and bad, sickness and health and for richer or for poorer."-I was promising to always be there and love her in every condition that we may go through or encounter.

"**I vow** to cherish you as an unending gift from God."-I promised to cherish her always because I know that the good Lord had favor on me and blessed me with the one gift that will keep on giving for the rest of my life! And that is my wife, Evangelist Rosalind L. Willis. Not only for the unconditional love that she gives to me and our children, but also to the people of this world. She has that agape love!

My vision for our marriage is for Rosalind and I, is to continue to love and cherish each other as we always have. But above else, be soldiers for Christ. Continue to do HIS WILL, by worshipping Him and being of service to others. Focusing on doing His business because if we continue to do that then we as a Union will be blessed and continue to remain "Self".

Rosalind's Revelation
"VOWS"

As you prepare for the marriage with your mate you must have a vision for your marriage and you both need to discuss it. For the word of God says "Can two walk together except they be agreed?" (Amos 3:3 KJV) Also (Proverbs 29:18) states: "Where there is no vision, the people perish: but he that kept the law, happy is he". I have experienced firsthand the difference between having a vision for marriage or just being married because that is the right thing to do. If you do not know the direction in which your marriage is going it will end up nowhere. You have to see yourself together walking in your God given Destiny!!!! If there is something that your spirit doesn't agree with, discuss it and make sure you get an understanding. Tommy set the template by the leading of the Holy spirit for these vows and I followed the standard that the Holy spirit set. I am going to do the same thing that my love did in this chapter. I will write my vows out in this section and explain why I wrote them and what vision I had when I wrote them:

"For as long as God continues to raise the morning sun, I will hold these vows sacred."-This was our main focus on both Tommy and I vows, because if we can't do this one sentence right here than anything after this doesn't even matter, this was the foundation. Because after this point any vow I write has to be kept deeply in my spirit where my love is concerned as long as I have breath in my body and the Lord Jesus blesses me to wake up each morning.

"**I vow to** love you with my mind, body, spirit. To be a caretaker of your inner man and to keep your name in God's ear."-I was promising my love that I will love him with every fiber of my being my entire self. And be there for him not only in the natural, but in the spiritual as well. And I will pray for him continuously with travail until Christ Jesus returns to receive us unto himself.

"**I vow to be** a productive confidant for your dreams and ambitions in life and to birth them into reality. To challenge you as I challenge myself so that we may continuously produce good fruit."-I was promising my love that I will productively be the one that he can confide in to carry in my womb his dreams and be that constant support system that will always reflect his destiny. And challenge him as well as myself to not get stagnant in life but to continue to PUSH all while bringing people to Christ, so that they may receive their relationship with Jesus, and step into their Divine destiny.

"**I vow to** be an everlasting source for our children so that they may come to me for a sense of direction and guidance. And provide them with love, knowledge, and understanding."-I promise to be there for **all our children** whenever they need someone to listen so that they may vent, or they need advice on just experiences in what they are walking through. I will pray continually and show them love, the knowledge and understanding of life and above all else be a consistent example in my walk with Christ Jesus.

"**I vow to** accept you, Self, Baby, my Handsome King as my lifetime mate, to believe in you and toil with you; not only in our finest hours, but in the midst of adversity as well. So that our connection through life will be of love and the inner peace of being loved."-I promise to accept Tommy as my husband until the Jesus returns to receive us unto himself. To believe in and support him and work with him and believe in him not only in our best of times, but in times of trouble as well. And always trusting in Jesus and his word while knowing that whatever we may face in life good or bad it will bring us closer by knowing that I love him and the peace of knowing that my depth of the love I have for him; he has that same depth of love for me.

"**I vow to** serve you as well as accepting of being served. To respect your thoughts, your sense of self-worth, the Godly Man that the good Lord called you to be and the sanctity of our marriage that He has so graciously blessed us with."-I was promising him that I will be honored to serve him as well as allowing him to serve me as a husband and wife should serve one another. To respect every part of him, and the sanctity of our marriage, and above all else the Mighty man of God that he is.

"**I vow to love** you and honor you with respect and admiration for you is a reflection of Christ Jesus and made in the image of God so I accept you and I will carry your favor as long as the blood continues to run in my veins. "-I was promising my love that I will honor and respect him.

"THE VISION FOR OUR MARRIAGE"
"Proverbs 29:18"

My vision for our marriage is for Tommy and me to continue to love and cherish each other as we always have. But above else, be examples and soldiers for Christ. Continue to do the WILL of the Father through Jesus by worshipping him, staying focused, and by being of service to others. To continue to walk in Divine Destiny focusing only on what we do for Christ for that is the only thing that will last. To not die with vision and purpose in our belly, but to birth out everything we were put here to do. We see our marriage as a gift from God so we give it back to him as a gift so that he can continually get all the Glory out of it. We want to see others experience the true meaning of marriage and all the blessings that it truly bring, in Jesus Name!

♥♥♥*Our Song* "*DESTINY*"♥♥♥
Written by Us

Tommy's Part ♥

Don't if feel good when I tell you that I love you?
And don't it feel good because you know my heart is true?
And don't it feel good cause you know I'll love you forever?
Oh it feels good when I am waking up next to you . . .
Because you're my first love
A match made in heaven above and
Baby you complete me with you I see clearly . . .
You are my DESTINY, the very best part of me
And with you is where I was always meant to be
Oh Baby, with you is where I was always meant to be . . .

Rosalind's Part ♥

Yes it feels good when you tell me that you love me.
And yes it feels good because I know your love is true.
Oh it feels good because I know you'll love forever
And it sure feels good waking up next to you
Because you're my first love
A match made in heaven above
Baby you complete me with you I see clearly
You are my DESTINY, the very best part of me
And with you is where I was created to be
Oh Baby with you is where I was always meant to be . . .

Our Prayer for Our Marriage

Heavenly Father,

We thank you for giving us your son Jesus Christ as an example of how we are to live in this life and eternity. We pray that our marriage will be a continual reflection of your Glory to empower and strengthen others by living and walking in this Divine Destiny that you set forth for us. We do not take it lightly that you chose us. We humbly ask you to continue to lead and direct us in your ways and not our own. We die to our will; and we say yes to your Divine will for our lives. In Jesus name we pray . . .

AMEN

ACKNOWLEDGMENTS

*-First and foremost we acknowledge God our Father and our Lord and Savior Jesus Christ as the head of our lives and the very breathe of our existence. Thank you for choosing us when we know you could have chosen anyone else to carry out this mandate. We humbly except the task at hand. Yes to **Your Will** Lord we Love You!*

— Elder Tyson and Jennifer Willis for coming into agreement with us and the Holy Spirit by bringing us together in holy matrimony. Jennifer thank you for cooking us our first meal as husband and wife, "delicious". We would like to thank both of you for opening up your home and hearts to receive us in this chapter of our lives. Thank you for being a Christian example in which you helped us to identify an example of a Godly marriage.

— Chris and Terry Quimbly. We thank you for opening your home and your hearts to us. Thank you for being so loving and supportive at all times. We cannot wait to see you guys again.

— Prophetess Sherry Castro. We thank you for your continual love and support in both word and deed. You are truly a blessing in our lives.

— Leona Theola, Mae Fields, for opening your home and heart as a gift of servant hood to receive our family with love and support we will forever be grateful. Thank you for being our beautician and sewing into us. We love you "Woosie"!

— My cousin Sonya, thank you for all ways being supportive and loving. You're my sister first and cousin second, I will forever love and appreciate you.

— Aunt Sylvia and Uncle Roosevelt for cooking us breakfast and giving us words of encouragement when it seem like we did not have a lot of support. We love you guys …

— Clarence and Stephanie Williams, for opening up your home with love and support while we were in transition. Thank you for your words of encouragement and for being there consistently, you are greatly appreciated more than words can explain.

— Minister Rodrick Chambers, for all the prayer and support. But above, all love that you have so humbly poured upon us. Thank you for being a consistent example of a Godly man, we appreciate you.

— Lisa Balonis, For being the coolest boss I've ever known. You were a gift in my time of need of knowing what my self-worth and sense of direction was. I thank you for being a mentor and someone I can look up to. We thank you for your patience and time when you didn't have to be. You are truly a blessing.

— Tonyette White, for being an instrumental part in bringing us together. Thank you for adding someone you did not know.

— Lisa Escobedo, Anna Lucero, Dan Hutchinson, Rebecca Chavez, Frank Gallegos, and Eva Martinez for your support, mentoring and a sense of direction and all of you for believing in me. I will forever be grateful.

— Anna Lucero, Dan Hutchinson, and Lisa Escobedo for your support, mentoring and a sense of direction. I will forever be grateful.

— Mr. and Mrs. Damon Willis, for being there in word and deed. Thank you for sowing into us when you two didn't have to. And making my Baby's first birthday as Mrs. Willis special. You are truly appreciated!

— Pastor Herbert and Co-Pastor Russell. Thank you for your prayers and support.

— To all of our siblings that names were not written above; we love you and appreciate you as well. "Lakeysha, Son, Tina, Glennis, Jeannie, Eric, Tonette, Annette, and Lynn.

— Face book family who have prayed for us and supported us.

OUR JEWELS

♥ CONTACT PAGE ♥

CONFERENCES, WORKSHOPS, PUBLIC SPEAKING EVENTS,
REVIVALS AND RETREATS

MINISTRY ADDRESS IS:
TOMMY & ROSALIND WILLIS
P.O. BOX 3561
ABILENE, TX. 79604
(325) 261-3875

www.birthingprocessministries@yahoo.com

REMEMBER: MARRIAGE IS MINISTRY!

Next book project:

IT'S ALL ABOUT DESTINY:
The Path To The Promise

www.ingramcontent.com/pod-product-compliance
Lightning Source LLC
Chambersburg PA
CBHW021303280526
45784CB00005B/2490